YOUR BASIC GUIDE TO THINGS THAT GO BUMP IN THE NIGHT

By E. Dagforth

Contents

Baba Yaga

Baba Yaga, the legendary figure from Slavic folklore, is a fascinating and enigmatic character that has captivated imaginations for centuries. Known as a powerful and unpredictable witch, Baba Yaga is often portrayed as an old hag with a long, bony nose, disheveled hair, and iron teeth. She lives deep in the heart of the forest, in a hut that stands on chicken legs and is surrounded by a fence made of human bones. The hut is said to move around at will, spinning and turning, making it difficult to locate or approach.

Baba Yaga is both feared and revered, as she possesses incredible knowledge of magic and is believed to hold the key to unlocking hidden wisdom and secrets. She is often depicted as a trickster, testing the character and determination of those who seek her help or cross her path. Her tests are often bizarre and challenging, requiring wit, courage, and resourcefulness to overcome. Those who fail her tests are met with punishment, while those who succeed are rewarded with her knowledge and sometimes even with a magical item or boon.

Legends and stories about Baba Yaga vary across different regions, but one common thread is her association with nature and the wilderness. She is seen as a guardian of the natural world, with a deep connection to the spirits of the forest, animals, and plants. It is said that she can communicate with animals and possesses the ability to shapeshift into various forms, such as a bird or a wolf, allowing her to move swiftly and unnoticed through the woods.

Baba Yaga is often sought out by those in need of her magical powers, whether it be to cure ailments, find lost treasures, or seek guidance on important matters. However, approaching her is no easy task, for she demands respect and will not tolerate foolishness or disrespect. To gain her favor, individuals must show humility, courage, and a pure heart.

Despite her often intimidating and fearsome nature, Baba Yaga also has a more complex side. In some stories, she is portrayed as a wise and benevolent figure, willing to help those who approach her with sincerity and respect. She has been known to provide advice and assistance to those who prove themselves worthy, acting as a mentor and guide.

The legend of Baba Yaga has become deeply ingrained in Slavic cultures and continues to inspire artists, writers, and filmmakers to this day. Her character has been featured in numerous folk tales, novels, and movies, each interpretation adding its own unique twist to the myth. As a symbol of feminine power, wisdom, and the forces of nature, Baba Yaga remains a compelling figure, embodying both darkness and light, and reminding us of the complexities of the human spirit.

Black Annis

Black Annis, a fearsome and legendary figure in English folklore, is a character surrounded by mystery and myth. Also known as Black Agnes or Black Anna, she is often depicted as a terrifying hag or witch, haunting the countryside and preying upon unsuspecting victims. The origins of Black Annis can be traced back to the Leicestershire region of England, particularly the city of Leicester, where her legend has been passed down through generations.

According to the tales, Black Annis was said to be an old woman with blue skin and long, sharp claws that she used to snatch and devour children who wandered too close to her lair. She was known to dwell in a cave or hollowed-out tree known as "Black Annis' Bower" on the outskirts of Leicester's Dane Hills. The bower was said to be made from the bones and skin of her victims, creating a gruesome and eerie atmosphere that struck fear into the hearts of the locals.

Legends surrounding Black Annis often depict her as a guardian of the land, fiercely territorial and protective of her territory. She was said to have a particular affinity for oak trees and would hide amongst their branches, waiting patiently for her next victim. It was believed that she had supernatural powers, such as shape-shifting into a monstrous cat-like creature, enabling her to move swiftly and silently in the night.

Her name, "Black Annis," is believed to have derived from her habit of dyeing her skin with a blue pigment extracted from a plant called woad, giving her a dark, almost black appearance. This practice not only added to her terrifying image but also served as a disguise, allowing her to blend into the shadows and strike fear into the hearts of those who dared to cross her path.

The legend of Black Annis has become deeply ingrained in the folklore of the region, serving as a cautionary tale to children and a reminder of the dangers that lurk in the darkness. Over the years, her story has evolved, taking on different variations and adaptations, but the essence of a malevolent and powerful figure remains consistent.

Today, Black Annis continues to capture the imagination of many, inspiring artwork, literature, and even appearing in modern media. She serves as a reminder of the power of folklore to shape and captivate our collective consciousness. Whether one believes in her existence or views her as merely a cautionary tale, Black Annis remains an enduring symbol of the supernatural, an embodiment of our deepest fears, and a testament to the rich tapestry of folklore that continues to enthrall us.

Black Dog/ Black Shuck

Black Dog or Black Shuck, as it is commonly known, is a legendary spectral hound that has been a subject of fascination and fear in various folklore and legends throughout history. This mysterious and ominous creature is often associated with tales of terror, haunting, and unfortunate encounters. The origins of the Black Dog myth can be traced back centuries, with sightings and accounts reported in different parts of the world, particularly in England, where it has left an indelible mark on local folklore.

One of the most enduring characteristics of Black Shuck is its appearance. It is often described as an enormous black dog, sometimes with glowing red or yellow eyes that seem to pierce through the darkness. Its size and features vary in different accounts, with some describing it as a massive creature towering over its victims, while others depict it as a more subtle and shadowy presence. Regardless of its specific form, the Black Dog exudes an aura of malevolence and foreboding.

Legends surrounding Black Shuck are filled with tales of its supernatural abilities and ominous occurrences. It is often associated with nighttime or stormy weather, appearing seemingly out of nowhere, instilling fear in those who cross its path. Accounts of Black Shuck haunting ancient crossroads, graveyards, or desolate landscapes are prevalent, further heightening the eerie nature of this spectral entity.

The encounters with Black Shuck are often described as harrowing experiences, with witnesses reporting feelings of extreme dread, a sense of impending doom, or even physical manifestations of its presence such as hair standing on end or sudden drops in temperature. Stories of the hound attacking or chasing individuals are widespread, leaving a lasting impression on those who have experienced or heard about such encounters.

Interestingly, the Black Dog legend has transcended folklore and made its mark in literature, art, and even popular culture. Authors such as Sir Arthur Conan Doyle, H.P. Lovecraft, and Sir Walter Scott have incorporated elements of the Black Dog myth into their works, further perpetuating its mystique. In the realm of art, paintings, sculptures, and illustrations have captured the essence of the Black Dog, adding to its enduring appeal as a subject of fascination.

While some consider Black Shuck to be purely a product of folklore and superstition, others believe that there may be deeper meaning and symbolism attached to this legendary creature. It is often associated with death, darkness, or otherworldly realms, serving as a metaphorical representation of the unknown and the fears that lurk within our subconscious minds.

Whether one believes in the physical existence of Black Shuck or views it as a symbol of our collective fears and anxieties, it remains an enduring and captivating figure in the annals of folklore. The tales of this spectral hound continue to intrigue and send shivers down the spines of those who dare to explore the realm of the supernatural. The legend of Black Dog offers a glimpse into the darker corners of our imagination and serves as a reminder of the power that folklore holds in shaping our cultural narratives.

Bogeyman

The Boogeyman, also spelled as Bogeyman, is an iconic figure deeply ingrained in folklore and legends across various cultures. The concept of the Boogeyman has fascinated and terrified people for centuries, serving as a cautionary tale to children and even adults. Let us delve into the captivating history and intriguing legends surrounding this mythical creature.

The origins of the Boogeyman can be traced back to ancient times when societies created supernatural beings to explain the unexplainable or to instill fear in individuals. In many cultures, the Boogeyman is believed to be a malevolent spirit or creature that preys on misbehaving children or those who disobey their parents. The name itself varies across cultures, with different regions referring to this figure by different names such as Babau, El Coco, Sack Man, or Raw Head and Bloody Bones.

One of the earliest mentions of the Boogeyman can be found in European folklore. In medieval times, parents would tell their children tales of a mysterious figure lurking in the shadows, waiting for disobedient children to snatch away and punish them. The Boogeyman was often described as a tall, dark figure, occasionally wearing a hooded cloak or carrying a sack to capture his victims. The fear of the unknown and the consequences of bad behavior became a powerful tool to ensure obedience and discipline among children.

As the concept of the Boogeyman spread to other cultures, it underwent various transformations, adapting to different societal beliefs and traditions. In African folklore, the Boogeyman takes the form of Mami Wata, a water spirit associated with both good fortune and misfortune. Mami Wata is depicted as a beautiful mermaid-like creature, luring unsuspecting victims into water bodies to drown them.

In Latin American folklore, the Boogeyman is known as El Coco, a creature often depicted as a ghostly figure or a monstrous humanoid with glowing eyes and sharp claws. El Coco is said to wander the streets at night, looking for disobedient children to abduct or devour. Parents would warn their children, saying, "Behave, or El Coco will come for you."

The Boogeyman has also made appearances in popular culture, particularly in literature, movies, and urban legends. In literature, the character of the Boogeyman has been featured in various works, such as Washington Irving's "The Legend of Sleepy Hollow" and Stephen King's "The Boogeyman." In movies, the Boogeyman often takes the form of a masked or supernatural killer, haunting the dreams or realities of unsuspecting victims.

While the Boogeyman's true existence remains a subject of debate and speculation, it continues to serve as a cautionary figure, reminding individuals, especially children, of the consequences of misbehavior and disobedience. Whether it is the chilling tales passed down through generations, the bedtime stories that send shivers down our spines, or the whispered warnings from parents, the Boogeyman remains an enduring and enigmatic figure that continues to capture our imagination.

In conclusion, the history and legends of the Boogeyman offer a fascinating glimpse into the collective psyche of cultures worldwide. This infamous creature embodies the fear of the unknown, retribution for wrongdoing, and the power of storytelling. Whether myth or reality, the Boogeyman remains an enduring symbol that reminds us to be mindful of our actions and to heed the lessons passed down through generations.

Bunyip

The bunyip, a legendary creature from Australian folklore, has fascinated and intrigued both locals and visitors for centuries. The origins of this mysterious creature can be traced back to the Indigenous Australian culture, where it holds a prominent place in their mythology and oral traditions. The bunyip is often described as a large, aquatic beast that inhabits rivers, swamps, and billabongs, making eerie sounds during the night, sending shivers down the spines of those who dare to listen.

The word "bunyip" itself is believed to have been derived from different Indigenous languages across Australia, with various interpretations of its meaning. In some tribes, it is associated with a powerful ancestral spirit or guardian of water bodies, while in others, it is seen as a malevolent creature that should be feared. This diversity in interpretations reflects the rich cultural diversity and vast landscapes of the Australian continent.

The stories and legends surrounding the bunyip have been passed down through generations, often serving as cautionary tales or explanations for natural phenomena. Indigenous communities have tales of people being taken by the bunyip, serving as warnings to avoid dangerous waterways or to exercise caution when venturing into unfamiliar territories. The creature's appearance and behavior vary in different accounts, with descriptions ranging from a monstrous, hulking beast with sharp claws and tusks, to a more mystical creature with the ability to change its form at will.

European settlers in Australia also encountered stories and sightings of the bunyip, which further fueled the creature's legend. As they explored the unknown wilderness, they encountered strange sounds, peculiar footprints, and eerie sightings that they attributed to this elusive creature. Many early settlers found solace in sharing their encounters, and tales of the bunyip quickly spread throughout colonial society.

In the 19th century, the bunyip transitioned from being a creature of Indigenous folklore to a creature of popular culture. It became a subject of interest for naturalists, explorers, and writers, who sought to understand and document Australia's unique fauna and folklore. The bunyip became a symbol of the mysterious and untamed Australian landscape, captivating the imaginations of both Australians and people from around the world.

As time went on, the bunyip's significance shifted from being a feared creature to becoming a beloved character in children's books, cartoons, and even tourism campaigns. It transformed from a creature of dread to a source of national pride, showcasing Australia's rich folklore and cultural heritage.

Today, the bunyip continues to capture the imagination of people worldwide. It represents the enduring connection between humans and the natural environment, reminding us of the mysteries and wonders that still exist in the world. Whether you believe in its existence or consider it a mythical creature, the bunyip remains an integral part of Australian folklore, keeping alive the stories and legends of the past while inspiring generations to come.

Changeling

Changelings are steeped in ancient folklore and legends. These creatures, often associated with fairies and other supernatural entities, have been the subject of countless tales passed down through generations. The concept of changelings can be traced back to various cultures and mythology, with each region offering its unique take on these enigmatic beings.

In European folklore, changelings were believed to be fairy creatures that would secretly replace human infants with their own kind. It was believed that fairies coveted human babies for their innocence and beauty, leaving behind a changeling in their place. These changelings were said to be sickly, mischievous, and often displayed peculiar behavior. Parents would often notice sudden changes in their child's demeanor, such as excessive crying, rapid aging, or abnormal physical characteristics, which were attributed to the presence of a changeling.

The legend of changelings served as a way for people to explain the sudden illnesses or disabilities that afflicted infants. In a time when medical knowledge was limited, changelings became a supernatural scapegoat for unexplained phenomena. Parents would go to great lengths to protect their children from being taken, resorting to various rituals and charms to ward off fairies and keep their homes safe.

In some cultures, it was believed that if a suspected changeling was discovered, certain actions could be taken to return the stolen child. Methods ranged from subjecting the changeling to physical harm, such as holding them above a fire or scalding them with hot water, to more gentle approaches like leaving the changeling out in the forest to entice the fairies to bring back the original child. These practices, though rooted in superstition and fear, highlight the lengths that people would go to reclaim their stolen children.

While changelings are primarily associated with European folklore, similar concepts can be found worldwide. In Irish mythology, for instance, the "sidhe" or fairy folk were believed to kidnap human infants and replace them with fairy children. In Scandinavian folklore, tales of trolls and goblins stealing human babies and leaving their own offspring behind were prevalent.

The belief in changelings, though largely seen as mythical in our modern era, offers a glimpse into the fears and anxieties of our ancestors. It reflects a time when the unexplainable was attributed to supernatural forces and serves as a reminder of our collective human need to make sense of the world around us.

Today, the concept of changelings continues to inspire writers, artists, and storytellers. From literature to popular culture, these mythical creatures have found their way into various forms of media, captivating audiences with their mysterious nature and ability to blur the lines between the human and supernatural realms.

Djinn

The Djinn, also known as Jinns or Genies, are mystical beings deeply rooted in the folklore and mythology of various cultures across the world, particularly in the Middle Eastern and Islamic traditions. These supernatural entities have captivated the imaginations of people for centuries, with stories and legends portraying them as powerful and enigmatic beings with the ability to grant wishes or wreak havoc.

The concept of Djinn traces back to ancient Arabian mythology, where they were believed to be created by God out of smokeless fire, existing parallel to humans and possessing free will. In Islamic theology, Djinn are considered sentient beings made from smokeless fire, invisible to the naked eye but capable of interacting with humans and influencing their lives. They are believed to inhabit a realm parallel to ours, with their own societies, hierarchies, and individual personalities.

Legends surrounding Djinn are diverse and rich, with numerous tales featuring their interactions with humans. While some portray Djinn as benevolent and helpful, others depict them as mischievous and malevolent beings, capable of manipulating and deceiving humans. It is said that they possess immense knowledge and supernatural powers, allowing them to shape-shift, teleport, and even possess individuals.

One famous tale involving Djinn is the story of Aladdin and the magic lamp. According to the Arabian Nights, a collection of Middle Eastern folktales, Aladdin stumbles upon a magic lamp containing a powerful Djinn who grants him three wishes. This story has become synonymous with the concept of Djinn and their ability to grant wishes, albeit with certain limitations and consequences.

In Islamic folklore, there are various classifications of Djinn, ranging from Marid (the most powerful and rebellious) to Ifrit (associated with fire and smoke) and Jinn (a broad term encompassing all Djinn). These classifications further emphasize the diverse nature of these supernatural entities.

Throughout history, Djinn have been associated with mysterious occurrences and unexplained phenomena. In ancient times, they were often blamed for diseases, possession, and other inexplicable events. People sought protection from Djinn through amulets, talismans, and rituals, as they were believed to have the ability to bring both good fortune and misfortune.

As knowledge and cultural exchange expanded over time, the concept of Djinn spread to different parts of the world, adapting and blending with local beliefs and traditions. In South Asian folklore, the concept of Djinn amalgamated with Hindu and Buddhist mythologies, resulting in a fusion of supernatural beings known as "Djinns" or "Diyas." Similarly, in Western culture, Djinn found their place in literature and popular culture, often depicted as magical beings capable of granting wishes, as seen in movies like "Aladdin" and "The Wishmaster."

Despite their widespread popularity, the understanding of Djinn remains deeply rooted in mythology and folklore. While some individuals believe in their existence and interact with them through spiritual practices, others consider Djinn as symbolic representations of human desires, struggles, and hidden potentials.

The legends surrounding Djinn reveal a captivating world of supernatural beings that have fascinated and intrigued people for centuries. Whether they are seen as benevolent or malevolent, the Djinn continue to inspire countless stories, sparking our imagination and reminding us of the vast mysteries that lie beyond our ordinary reality.

Doppelganger

Doppelgangers, also known as "double walkers," are eerie and mysterious entities. The concept of a doppelganger refers to a supernatural phenomenon where a person has an exact look-alike or double, often seen as a harbinger of misfortune or a symbol of impending doom. The origins of doppelganger lore can be traced back to ancient civilizations and are deeply intertwined with folklore, mythology, and literature.

One of the earliest mentions of doppelgangers can be found in Norse mythology, with the mythological figure of the Vardøger. According to Norse folklore, the Vardøger is a spiritual entity that precedes an individual, performing actions identical to those of the person it mimics. This phenomenon would often leave witnesses perplexed, believing they had encountered the actual person before their arrival. Similar beliefs can be found in other cultures around the world, such as the Celtic fetch and the Germanic doppelgänger.

In German folklore, doppelgangers are believed to be supernatural doubles or mirror images that inhabit the earthly realm. They are often portrayed as malicious entities, bearing an ill omen or representing an impending tragedy. Seeing one's own doppelganger was believed to be a sign of imminent death. Famous historical figures such as Johann Wolfgang von Goethe and Percy Bysshe Shelley claimed to have encountered their doppelgangers, further adding to the mystique surrounding these enigmatic beings.

Literature has also played a significant role in perpetuating the legends and fascination with doppelgangers. In Fyodor Dostoevsky's novel "The Double," the protagonist encounters a doppelganger who gradually takes over his life, leading to his descent into madness. Edgar Allan Poe's short story "William Wilson" explores the theme of a doppelganger as a symbol of one's conscience or alter ego. These literary works have contributed to the enduring appeal and exploration of doppelgangers in popular culture.

Psychologically, the phenomenon of doppelgangers has been linked to the concept of the "uncanny." This Freudian term refers to a feeling of unease or discomfort when encountering something that appears familiar yet also strangely unfamiliar. The sight of a doppelganger can trigger this unsettling sensation, as the human mind struggles to reconcile the presence of an exact replica.

In modern times, doppelgangers have become a popular trope in various forms of media, including movies, television shows, and even social media. The notion of a doppelganger has evolved beyond being a mere harbinger of doom and has been reimagined in various ways, often as a source of intrigue, curiosity, or even humor. The concept has been exploited in stories of mistaken identities, clones, and parallel universes, sparking thought-provoking narratives and exploring the human fascination with the self and identity.

Goblins

Goblins, those mischievous and often malevolent creatures of folklore. With their grotesque appearance, cunning nature, and penchant for causing trouble, goblins have become a staple in mythologies and legends around the world.

The origin of goblins can be traced back to ancient European folklore. In these tales, goblins were often depicted as small, grotesque creatures with leathery skin, pointed ears, and sharp teeth. They were believed to dwell in dark places such as caves, forests, and abandoned mines, emerging only at night to wreak havoc on unsuspecting humans.

In Norse mythology, goblins were known as "trolls," notorious for their strength, ill-intent, and stone-like appearance. These trolls were feared by humans and were said to turn to stone when exposed to sunlight. In Scandinavian folklore, goblins were believed to be the spirits of deceased children who had not been baptized, and their mischievous behavior was seen as a result of their restless souls.

In English folklore, goblins were often associated with household chores and were thought to be responsible for untidiness and general disorder. They were said to move objects, hide belongings, and create general chaos within households. This belief led to the tradition of leaving out offerings such as milk or bread to appease the goblins and keep them from causing mayhem.

Goblins also played a significant role in Celtic mythology. In Irish folklore, goblins were known as "puca" or "pooka." These shapeshifting creatures were known for their ability to transform into various animals such as horses, cats, or goats. They were believed to be tricksters who would lead unsuspecting travelers astray or steal their belongings. Despite their mischievous nature, goblins were also known to possess magical abilities and were sometimes sought out for their knowledge of healing herbs and potions.

Throughout history, goblins have been portrayed as cunning and treacherous creatures, often serving as antagonists in various fairy tales and legends. From the Brothers Grimm's tale of "The Elves and the Shoemaker" to J.R.R. Tolkien's depiction of goblins in "The Hobbit," these creatures have become synonymous with mischief, danger, and the supernatural.

In modern popular culture, goblins continue to be a prevalent theme in literature, films, and games. They are often depicted as adversaries to brave heroes, lurking in the shadows and waiting to cause trouble. Their notoriety has even extended into the realm of fantasy role-playing games, where goblins are frequently encountered as low-level foes that players must overcome on their quests.

The enduring fascination with goblins can be attributed to their ability to tap into our primal fears and our enduring curiosity about the supernatural. Whether they are portrayed as malevolent tricksters or as misunderstood creatures, goblins have left an indelible mark on our collective imagination.

So, next time you hear a strange noise in the dark or misplace an item without explanation, remember the legends and tales of goblins that have shaped our perception of these mysterious creatures. While we may never truly know if goblins exist beyond the realm of myth and folklore, their enduring presence in our stories and legends is a testament to their power to captivate and terrify us.

Gremlins

Gremlins are mischievous and elusive creatures whose origins can be traced back to a fascinating history and a myriad of legends.

The concept of gremlins originated during World War II within the British Royal Air Force. Aviation technology was still in its infancy, and mechanical failures were common. To explain these inexplicable malfunctions, pilots and engineers began blaming gremlins - supernatural creatures believed to sabotage aircraft. Gremlins were depicted as small, impish beings with an affinity for tinkering with machinery, often leading to dangerous consequences.

Legends of gremlins date back even further, with similar creatures appearing in folklore and mythology around the world. In English folklore, gremlins were known as mischievous household spirits. They were believed to inhabit homes and cause disturbances such as moving or hiding objects, creating strange noises, or even damaging property.

Interestingly, the name "gremlin" itself has uncertain origins. Some speculate that it may have derived from the Old English word "gremian," meaning "to vex" or "to annoy." Others suggest it could have come from the Old German word "greme," meaning "fury" or "anger." Regardless of its etymology, the term "gremlin" has become synonymous with these vexing and troublesome creatures.

The stories and legends surrounding gremlins have taken various forms over time. They have been depicted as tiny creatures with wings, similar to fairies or sprites, or as small, goblin-like creatures with pointed ears and mischievous grins. Gremlins are often portrayed as playful troublemakers, enjoying causing havoc and chaos wherever they go.

In popular culture, the concept of gremlins has been widely embraced. The 1984 film, "Gremlins," directed by Joe Dante, brought these creatures to the forefront of mainstream media. The movie introduced Gizmo, a cute and innocent creature, and the destructive, mischievous gremlins that emerged from him when certain rules were broken.

Since then, gremlins have become a staple in literature, films, and even video games, captivating audiences with their unique blend of chaos and charm. They have become icons of mischief, embodying the allure of the unknown, and the dangers that may arise when human inventions and supernatural forces intersect.

The enduring fascination with gremlins can be attributed to their ability to tap into our collective fear of the unknown and our desire to explain the unexplainable. They serve as a reminder that, despite our advancements in technology, there are still forces beyond our control that can disrupt our lives.

So, whether you believe in the existence of gremlins as actual supernatural beings or simply enjoy their presence in popular culture, the allure of these mischievous creatures continues to captivate and entertain us. Their legends and stories, rooted in history and folklore, have left an indelible mark on our imaginations, making gremlins an enduring part of our cultural mythology.

Imps

Mischievous and often misunderstood supernatural beings, Imps have a rich history rooted in folklore and legends spanning across different cultures and time periods. These pint-sized creatures are believed to possess magical abilities and are often associated with pranks, tricks, and even acts of malevolence. From ancient mythology to modern-day tales, the concept of imps has captivated the imaginations of people worldwide. Let us embark on a journey to explore the fascinating history and legends surrounding these enigmatic entities.

The origin of the word "imp" can be traced back to the Old English word "impa," meaning a young shoot or a sapling. In folklore, imps are often depicted as small, supernatural beings associated with the devil or other malevolent forces. They are commonly described as small, human-like creatures with demonic features such as horns, tails, and bat-like wings. Despite their diminutive size, imps are believed to possess immense powers and magical abilities.

In ancient Greek and Roman mythology, the concept of imps can be seen in the form of mischievous spirits known as "daimones." These entities were associated with various aspects of life, such as fertility, luck, and even death. From Pan, the mischievous satyr-like deity, to Puck, the clever and playful trickster in Shakespeare's "A Midsummer Night's Dream," imps have long been intertwined with folklore and mythology.

In medieval Europe, imps took on a more sinister reputation. They were often portrayed as familiars, serving witches and sorcerers in their dark practices. According to popular belief, these imps were said to be summoned by witches through dark rituals or pacts made with the devil. They were thought to aid in carrying out wicked deeds or causing havoc in the lives of unsuspecting individuals.

Legends surrounding imps vary greatly in different cultures. In Germanic folklore, there is a creature known as a "Kobold," which bears a resemblance to imps. Kobolds were believed to reside in houses, mines, or other places and would either help or hinder the human inhabitants, depending on their treatment. They were known to cause mischief by hiding objects, making noises, or even causing accidents.

In Scottish folklore, there is the legendary creature known as the "Brownie." Brownies were small, helpful imps who would perform domestic tasks in houses. They would discreetly complete chores and bring good fortune to those who treated them with respect and kindness. However, if mistreated or neglected, they could become mischievous and cause trouble.

In modern times, imps have become popular characters in literature, films, and video games. From the mischievous "Imps" in the iconic game "Doom" to the lovable "Imp" character in the animated movie "Onward," these fantastical beings continue to capture our imaginations.

Whether seen as mischievous troublemakers or helpful companions, the history and legends of imps have intrigued and fascinated generations. They serve as a reminder of the enduring human fascination with the supernatural and the role these mystical creatures play in our collective imagination.

To delve deeper into the realm of imps and discover ancient remedies and modern therapies for preventing headaches, download our comprehensive e-book on headache therapies. Packed with valuable information and practical tips, this e-book will empower you to take control of your headaches and live a life free from their torment. Don't miss out on this opportunity to gain valuable insights and find relief. Download our e-book today and bid farewell to those pesky headaches!

Incubus/Succubus

Both of these creatures are believed to infiltrate the dreams and desires of humans, often with seductive and sometimes terrifying consequences. The origins of these entities can be traced back to ancient folklore and mythology, spanning across cultures and civilizations.

The term "Incubus" is derived from the Latin word "incubus," meaning "to lie upon." In various cultures, an Incubus is described as a male demon or spirit that visits women while they sleep, engaging in sexual relations and feeding off their life force. Similarly, a Succubus, derived from the Latin word "succuba," meaning "strumpet," is a female demon or spirit that preys on men in their dreams, draining their vitality.

The legends of these beings date back to ancient Mesopotamia, with similar accounts appearing in other ancient civilizations such as Sumer, Assyria, and Babylon. In these early tales, the Incubus and Succubus were believed to be nocturnal demons, often associated with Lilith, a female demon who tempted men in their sleep. Lilith became renowned as the queen of the Succubi, perpetuating the notion of these demonic seductresses.

In medieval Europe, during the time of the witchcraft hysteria, the belief in Incubi and Succubi reached its peak. These entities were considered as nocturnal visitors who engaged in sexual intercourse with individuals, often leaving them feeling exhausted, drained, and even traumatized. The Catholic Church played a significant role in perpetuating these beliefs, associating the experiences with witchcraft, sin, and demonic possession.

Throughout the centuries, countless stories and accounts have been shared, detailing encounters with these supernatural beings. Some believed that encounters with an Incubus or Succubus were a result of sleep paralysis, a state in which a person is temporarily unable to move or speak while falling asleep or waking up. This phenomenon, combined with vivid dreams and hallucinations, could easily be interpreted as encounters with these otherworldly creatures.

In more recent times, psychological and scientific explanations have been offered to demystify the legends of the Incubus and Succubus. Experts suggest that phenomena such as sleep paralysis, lucid dreaming, and sexual dreams can account for the experiences people attribute to these entities. However, the allure and fear associated with these mythical creatures continue to captivate the human imagination, inspiring literature, art, and popular culture.

In literature, authors like Johann Wolfgang von Goethe and H.P. Lovecraft have explored the theme of the Incubus and Succubus, delving into the psychological and supernatural aspects of these beings. In popular culture, films, television shows, and video games have depicted these entities, often portraying them as seductive and malevolent creatures.

Mermen

Mermen are the male counterparts of the mythical creatures known as mermaids. They are often depicted as half-human, half-fish, possessing the upper body of a man and the lower body of a fish. While mermaids have gained more attention in popular culture, the legends and lore surrounding mermen are equally fascinating. Let us embark on a journey through the history and legends of these aquatic beings, exploring the tales that have made mermen an enduring part of folklore.

The concept of mermen can be traced back to various ancient civilizations around the world. In ancient Greece, the sea god Poseidon is often depicted as a bearded merman, ruling over the oceans and commanding the power of the seas. In Norse mythology, the sea god Njord is depicted as a merman, associated with wealth, fertility, and the protection of seafarers. These early depictions of mermen showcase their association with the sea and their connection to the divine.

Legends surrounding mermen often portray them as alluring and mysterious beings, capable of captivating sailors and luring them beneath the waves. In these tales, mermen are said to possess enchanting voices, capable of singing haunting melodies that bewitch any who hear them. It is believed that those who succumb to the allure of a merman's song are doomed to a watery grave. These legends serve as cautionary tales, warning of the dangers that lie beneath the surface of the sea.

While mermen are often associated with danger, there are also stories that paint them in a more benevolent light. Some legends speak of mermen as protectors of the ocean and its inhabitants. It is said that they possess the ability to calm storms, guide lost sailors to safety, and bestow good fortune upon those who show them kindness. These depictions highlight the complex nature of mermen, representing both the power and mystery of the ocean, as well as their potential for benevolence.

In addition to the legends, mermen have also found their place in various works of art and literature throughout history. Paintings, sculptures, and literature often depict mermen as handsome and muscular beings, evoking a sense of strength and grace. The allure of mermen has inspired countless artists to capture their mystique, immortalizing them in visual form.

In contemporary culture, the fascination with mermen continues to thrive. From fantasy novels to films and television shows, mermen have become a popular subject, captivating audiences with their extraordinary existence. Their representation has evolved, showcasing a diverse range of interpretations, from romantic heroes to complex anti-heroes.

The legends and history of mermen have endured through time, captivating the imaginations of countless individuals. Whether viewed as alluring creatures of the deep or powerful guardians of the sea, mermen continue to captivate with their unique blend of beauty, mystery, and danger. As tales of mermen are passed down from generation to generation, we are reminded of the enduring power of mythology and the enchantment it brings to our lives.

Momo

Momo is the name given to a mysterious and haunting figure that gained international attention in 2018, originating from an eerie sculpture created by a Japanese special effects company, which later became an internet urban legend and a chilling viral phenomenon. The story behind Momo is shrouded in controversy and uncertainty, with many conflicting narratives and interpretations swirling around its origins and intentions. However, despite the ambiguity, Momo has undeniably left an indelible mark on popular culture and has become a cautionary tale for the modern digital age.

The birth of Momo can be traced back to a sculpture called "Mother Bird," which was crafted by Link Factory, a Japanese special effects company. The sculpture features a woman's head with long black hair, bulging eyes, and a wide, distorted grin. Its unsettling appearance and uncanny features set the stage for the terrifying character that emerged from its image.

In 2016, a photograph of the sculpture was shared on social media, capturing the attention of netizens and sparking a wave of curiosity and fascination. As the picture began to circulate online, various stories and legends started to emerge, associating the sculpture with supernatural abilities and malevolent intentions. The creepy image soon became synonymous with a disturbing internet challenge that purportedly encouraged self-harm and provoked vulnerable individuals into dangerous behavior.

The prominence of Momo reached its zenith in 2018 when it was linked to a series of viral WhatsApp messages and YouTube videos that allegedly contained hidden threats and commands from the monstrous character. Reports claimed that children were being targeted and coerced into performing harmful acts, further amplifying the panic and hysteria surrounding Momo's influence.

However, it is important to note that concrete evidence linking Momo to actual harm or malicious intent is scarce. Investigations into the phenomenon revealed that the most severe claims were largely unfounded, and the panic surrounding Momo was fueled by sensationalism and moral panic. Some argue that the Momo Challenge was primarily an empty threat, while others point to its potential harm as an urban legend that can psychologically impact susceptible individuals.

Nonetheless, the character's unnerving image quickly became an icon of fear, inspiring countless internet memes, artwork, and even Halloween costumes. Momo's eerie presence has transcended its original context, demonstrating the potency of viral scares and the speed at which urban legends can captivate the collective imagination.

Momo continues to serve as a reminder of the dark side of the internet and the potential dangers lurking behind the screen. Its story serves as a cautionary tale, highlighting the need for digital literacy, responsible online behavior, and the importance of maintaining open communication with children and vulnerable individuals.

Mothman and the MIB

Originating in Point Pleasant, West Virginia, the Mothman is described as a tall, winged humanoid with glowing red eyes. Its appearances are often associated with a sense of impending doom and tragedy. While the Mothman's story may seem like a terrifying urban legend, it has gained significant attention due to its alleged encounters with the enigmatic Men In Black.

The first documented sighting of the Mothman occurred on November 12, 1966. Five men were digging a grave in a local cemetery when they claimed to have seen a large creature fly directly over their heads. Following this initial encounter, numerous other residents of Point Pleasant reported seeing a similar winged creature. Witnesses described it as standing around six to seven feet tall, with a wingspan of ten feet or more. The sightings continued for over a year, creating a sense of fear and intrigue within the community.

As the sightings increased, the Mothman gained widespread attention, attracting media coverage and curious visitors to Point Pleasant. However, alongside the Mothman's appearances, another mysterious phenomenon emerged – encounters with the Men In Black. Described as individuals dressed in black suits, often driving black cars, these figures would show up after Mothman sightings or visit witnesses who had come forward with their experiences.

The Men In Black, as described by witnesses, were unsettling and otherworldly. They had pale complexions, strange manners, and an uncanny ability to gather detailed information about the Mothman sightings and those who witnessed them. Witnesses reported experiencing strange occurrences, such as electrical disturbances or missing time, after their encounters with the Men In Black. Some even claimed to have been threatened or intimidated into silence.

The relationship between the Mothman and the Men In Black remains unclear. Some theories suggest that the Men In Black were government agents attempting to cover up evidence of the Mothman's existence, while others propose that they may have been extraterrestrial beings monitoring the creature. The Mothman itself is often considered a harbinger of disaster, as its appearances were linked to the tragic collapse of the Silver Bridge on December 15, 1967, which claimed the lives of 46 people.

Despite the passage of time, the Mothman of Point Pleasant continues to captivate the imagination of believers and skeptics alike. The legend has inspired books, documentaries, and even a Hollywood film. The sightings and encounters remain a subject of speculation and debate, with some attributing the Mothman to a hoaxed creature or misidentified animals, while others firmly believe in its existence.

Whether one chooses to view the Mothman as a terrifying omen or a mere figment of imagination, its story intertwines with the mysterious Men In Black, creating a captivating narrative that continues to intrigue and fascinate those who delve into the realm of the unexplained.

Ogres

Ogres, mythical creatures of folklore and legend, have terrified people for centuries. From their origins in ancient mythology to their portrayal in popular culture, ogres have left their mark on our imaginations. In this exploration of their history and folklore, we will delve deep into the origins of ogres, their characteristics, and the stories that have woven their way into our collective consciousness.

The concept of the ogre can be traced back to ancient Mesopotamian mythology, where they were depicted as powerful and fearsome creatures. In the epic of Gilgamesh, the hero encounters an ogre named Humbaba, who guards the Cedar Forest. Humbaba is described as a monstrous creature with a terrifying visage, capable of instilling fear in any who lay their eyes upon him. This early representation of ogres as formidable beings set the foundation for their portrayal in later folklore.

As time went on, ogres found their way into various cultures and mythologies around the world. In European folklore, they were often described as large, brutish beings with an insatiable appetite for human flesh. These ogres were often depicted as living in remote and dangerous places such as forests or mountains, lurking in the shadows and preying on unsuspecting travelers. Some stories even told of ogres who possessed magical powers or could shape-shift into other forms to lure their victims.

One famous example of ogres in folklore is found in Charles Perrault's fairy tale "Hop-o'-My-Thumb." In this story, the titular character and his siblings are captured by a cannibalistic ogre after being abandoned by their parents. Hop-o'-My-Thumb outsmarts the ogre and manages to escape, ultimately leading to the ogre's demise. This tale, like many others featuring ogres, serves as a cautionary tale and emphasizes the triumph of wit and cleverness against seemingly insurmountable odds.

In addition to European folklore, ogres also feature prominently in Asian mythology. In Japanese folklore, there is a creature known as the oni, which shares similarities with the Western concept of ogres. Oni are often depicted as grotesque, horned creatures with a menacing appearance. They are believed to be malevolent beings, associated with natural disasters and misfortune. However, in some stories, oni can also be portrayed as protectors or guardians, showcasing the complex nature of these legendary creatures.

Throughout history, ogres have been used as metaphors and symbols, representing various aspects of human nature and societal fears. They have been seen as embodiments of gluttony, greed, and the darker side of humanity. As such, ogres have been used in literature and art to explore themes of morality, temptation, and the struggle between good and evil.

In modern times, ogres have gained widespread recognition through popular culture, most notably in the character of Shrek from the animated film franchise. Shrek, despite being an ogre, defies the traditional narrative by being a sympathetic and relatable character. This portrayal has helped reshape the image of ogres in contemporary storytelling, showing that they can possess depth and complexity beyond their monstrous appearances.

Rakshasa

The Rakshasa, often depicted as malevolent and powerful beings, hold a significant place in the rich tapestry of Indian folklore and mythology. The term "Rakshasa" originates from the Sanskrit word "raksha," which means "to protect" or "to guard." However, these creatures are far from the protectors one might envision. Rakshasas are often portrayed as shape-shifting demons or wicked spirits with a penchant for causing chaos and suffering.

In Hindu mythology, the Rakshasas are believed to be descendants of the sage Pulastya, one of the ten Prajapatis (mind-born sons of Brahma). Their origins can be traced back to the famous epic Ramayana, where they play prominent antagonistic roles. It is said that Rakshasas were created by Brahma to counterbalance the growing power of Devas (celestial beings) and intervened in human affairs, often causing havoc and torment.

According to various legends, Rakshasas possess incredible physical strength, magical abilities, and the power to change their forms to deceive and terrify their victims. They are known to dwell in dense forests, mountains, and dark and desolate places, emerging under the cover of darkness to terrorize unsuspecting travelers or disturb rituals and ceremonies.

Rakshasas are notorious for their insatiable appetite for flesh and blood. Tales speak of their preference for human flesh, often preying on solitary wanderers or lost individuals, luring them into their lairs with enchanting voices or grotesque illusions. Some Rakshasas are even portrayed as formidable sorcerers, capable of casting powerful spells and curses to manipulate and control humans.

In Hindu folklore, Rakshasas are not just portrayed as malevolent creatures but are also known for their complexity. Some stories depict them as tragic figures, cursed by the gods or driven to wickedness due to their own personal struggles. The epic Mahabharata features Rakshasas like Hidimba and her brother Hidimba, who ultimately find redemption through their interactions with the Pandavas.

Rakshasas are not exclusive to Hindu mythology; they have also found their way into other cultures and belief systems. In Buddhism, Rakshasas are seen as supernatural beings with a propensity for violence and aggression, often representing inner demons and obstacles on the path to enlightenment. In Southeast Asian folklore, they are known as "Yaksha" and are considered powerful nature spirits associated with trees, mountains, and water bodies.

The tales of Rakshasas have captivated generations, serving as cautionary tales, metaphorical representations, and embodiments of our fears and desires. Their role in folklore has been versatile, reflecting the complexity of human nature and the eternal struggle between good and evil. While they may be terrifying and malevolent, Rakshasas continue to intrigue us, reminding us of the importance of courage, resilience, and the triumph of righteousness over darkness.

Sirens

In Greek mythology, Sirens were enchanting creatures with the upper body of a woman and the lower body of a bird. Often depicted with beautiful voices, they would lure unsuspecting sailors to their demise with their irresistible songs. The origin of Sirens dates back to ancient Greek literature, where they were first mentioned in Homer's epic poem, the Odyssey.

According to the Odyssey, the Sirens resided on a rocky island, surrounded by treacherous waters. Their enchanting melodies were said to be so mesmerizing that sailors would become entranced, steering their ships toward the sirens' island, ultimately crashing against the rocks and meeting a tragic fate. These mythical creatures symbolize the irresistible temptations that can lead individuals astray, highlighting the dangers of succumbing to one's desires without caution or self-control.

The Sirens' allure extended beyond Greek mythology and found its way into various folklore and legends throughout different cultures. In ancient Rome, for instance, they were known as "Harpyiae" and were portrayed with the torso of a woman and the wings of a vulture. The Harpyiae were considered agents of retribution, punishing individuals who had committed heinous acts. Their role shifted from seductresses to avengers, reflecting the evolving interpretations of these intriguing mythical beings.

Over time, the image of the Sirens has also permeated art, literature, and popular culture. Numerous artworks, such as paintings and sculptures, have depicted the alluring and dangerous nature of the Sirens. In literature, the concept of the Siren has been utilized metaphorically to represent temptation or seduction, transcending the boundaries of their mythological origins. This enduring fascination with the Sirens speaks to their enduring impact on our collective consciousness.

While the Sirens may be mythical creatures, their symbolism and cautionary tales endure to this day. They remind us of the power of seduction, the importance of self-control, and the consequences that may arise from succumbing to our inner desires without exercising caution. In a modern context, the Sirens can serve as a metaphor for the various temptations and distractions that we encounter in our daily lives, reminding us to stay vigilant and not let ourselves be lured away from our intended path.

These enchanting creatures, with their captivating songs and irresistible allure, have fascinated and inspired generations. From the pages of ancient epics to the canvases of master artists, the Sirens continue to capture our imagination. Whether viewed as seductresses or agents of retribution, their stories and symbolism remind us of the dangers of unchecked desires and the importance of self-control. The legacy of the Sirens serves as a timeless reminder to navigate the treacherous waters of life with caution, lest we become ensnared by their enchanting calls.

Skinwalker

The Navajo Skinwalker, also known as *yee naaldlooshii*, is a creature deeply rooted in the mythology and folklore of the Navajo people, one of the largest indigenous tribes in the United States. The term "skinwalker" refers to a person with the supernatural ability to transform themselves into an animal, often for malevolent purposes. The legends surrounding the Navajo Skinwalker are both intriguing and haunting, offering a glimpse into the rich cultural heritage of the Navajo nation.

In Navajo tradition, the Skinwalker is believed to be a witch or sorcerer who has gained the power to shapeshift. These individuals are said to possess great knowledge of dark magic and are able to harness the spirits of animals to carry out their nefarious deeds. It is important to note that not all witches or sorcerers in Navajo culture are considered Skinwalkers, as most adhere to positive and beneficial practices.

The origins of the Skinwalker are deeply rooted in Navajo history and spirituality. According to Navajo belief, in order to acquire the power of transformation, a person must commit a terrible act, such as killing a close family member, to obtain the necessary supernatural abilities. This act of evil is said to sever their connection with the Navajo people and the sacredness of their land.

The Skinwalker is often described as a creature with the ability to take on various animal forms, including wolves, coyotes, owls, or crows. It is believed that they use these forms to commit acts of malevolence, such as inflicting sickness or death upon others. The Navajo people deeply fear encounters with Skinwalkers, as they are believed to possess the ability to manipulate thoughts, cause hallucinations, or even control the actions of their victims.

Encounters with Skinwalkers are considered rare and are often associated with an eerie sense of foreboding. They are said to possess glowing, animal-like eyes and emit a foul odor. Many Navajo people believe that they can detect the presence of a Skinwalker through certain signs, such as hearing strange noises outside their homes, experiencing unexplained illnesses, or witnessing animals behaving abnormally.

Navajo traditions provide various methods of protection against Skinwalkers. These include the use of sacred herbs, such as sage and cedar, as well as creating protective symbols or "medicine bags" containing items believed to ward off evil spirits. Additionally, ceremonies and rituals are performed to cleanse and protect individuals or homes from the malevolent influence of Skinwalkers.

While the Skinwalker remains a prominent figure in Navajo folklore, it is important to approach the topic with cultural sensitivity and respect. The stories and beliefs surrounding the Skinwalker are deeply intertwined with Navajo spirituality and the cultural identity of the Navajo people. It is crucial to understand and honor the significance of these traditions when exploring the history and folklore of the Skinwalker.

The Skinwalker is a captivating and complex figure in Native American folklore. Rooted in Navajo history and spirituality, this creature represents the dark side of human nature and serves as a reminder of the importance of maintaining balance and harmony within the world. The tales of the Skinwalker not only provide intrigue and chills but also offer a glimpse into the rich cultural heritage of the Navajo people, highlighting the profound connection they have with the natural world and the spiritual realm.

Slenderman

The Slenderman is a chilling and enigmatic figure that has become a modern-day legend. Born in the depths of internet folklore, this tall, faceless entity has infiltrated popular culture, inspiring horror stories, video games, and even a real-life tragedy. The story of the Slenderman is a fascinating blend of urban myth, online collaboration, and the power of storytelling.

The origins of the Slenderman can be traced back to a forum thread on the website Something Awful in 2009. Eric Knudsen, using the pseudonym Victor Surge, posted two photoshopped images that featured a tall, thin figure lurking in the background. Accompanied by brief captions, these images sparked immediate intrigue and curiosity among forum users. The character was described as a supernatural being with the ability to manipulate minds, abduct children, and instill fear in those who encountered it.

What made the Slenderman unique was the collaborative nature of its creation. Inspired by Knudsen's original posts, other users began adding their own stories, images, and videos, expanding the mythos around the character. This decentralized and collective storytelling approach allowed for a constant evolution of the Slenderman's narrative. It grew beyond its creator's initial vision and took on a life of its own as people added their own interpretations, experiences, and encounters with the entity.

As the Slenderman's popularity spread, it transcended the confines of online forums and emerged in various forms of media. Creepypasta stories, a genre of horror fiction circulated on the internet, embraced the Slenderman as a recurring theme. Writers and artists contributed to the ever-growing lore, crafting chilling tales that blurred the lines between reality and fiction. It was through these stories that the Slenderman became deeply ingrained in pop culture, capturing the attention of horror enthusiasts and curious readers alike.

However, the Slenderman's influence and impact reached a tragic turning point in 2014 when two 12-year-old girls, influenced by the fictional character, attempted to murder a classmate in Wisconsin. The incident shocked the world, raising complex questions about the blurred boundaries between fiction and reality, the impact of internet culture on vulnerable individuals, and the responsibility of creators and communities in fostering a safe online environment.

Despite the dark incident that became associated with the Slenderman, it is crucial to remember that the character itself is a work of fiction. It represents the power of storytelling, the allure of the unknown, and the fascination humans have with the macabre. The Slenderman continues to thrive in various forms, from video games like "Slender: The Eight Pages" to the 2018 feature film "Slender Man," solidifying its place in contemporary horror culture.

In summary, the story behind the Slenderman is a testament to the collaborative nature of online storytelling. From its humble beginnings on a forum thread, it has grown into a modern-day legend that continues to captivate and terrify audiences. Its influence, both positive and negative, serves as a reminder of the impact stories can have on our collective consciousness. Whether it is through cautionary tales or thrilling adventures, the Slenderman reminds us of the enduring power of the human imagination.

Wendigo

The Wendigo is a chilling creature deeply rooted in the folklore and legends of Native American tribes, particularly those from the Algonquian-speaking people of the northern United States and Canada. This monstrous figure has long captivated the imaginations of storytellers, serving as a cautionary tale and a symbol of the primal darkness that lurks within the human psyche.

The history of the Wendigo stretches back centuries, its origins shrouded in mystery and passed down through oral tradition. According to legend, the Wendigo was once a human being, transformed into a cannibalistic monster due to famine, greed, or resorting to the unspeakable act of cannibalism. This transformation was believed to be a curse, inflicted upon those who violated the sacred laws of their tribes or were consumed by insatiable desires.

The appearance of the Wendigo varies across different tribal accounts, but there are common elements that persist. Descriptions often depict a towering, emaciated figure, with elongated limbs and jagged, yellowed teeth. Its eyes burn with a malevolent hunger, and its skin clings tightly to its skeletal frame. Some believe that the Wendigo can change its size at will, growing larger or smaller to fit its surroundings, making it a formidable and elusive foe.

In Native American folklore, the Wendigo is associated with winter, famine, and the desolation of the wilderness. It is said to roam through the forests and icy landscapes, whispering its chilling cries that echo through the night. Some believe that the Wendigo possesses the ability to mimic human voices, luring unsuspecting victims deeper into the wilderness, where it can feast upon their flesh and absorb their life force.

Legends surrounding the Wendigo serve as a cautionary tale, warning against the dangers of greed, gluttony, and the loss of humanity. It represents the darkest aspects of human nature, the insatiable hunger that can consume individuals and drive them to commit unspeakable acts. The Wendigo embodies the fear of becoming disconnected from one's community, losing touch with empathy and morality, and succumbing to the temptations of the forbidden.

In recent years, the Wendigo has also found its way into popular culture, appearing in literature, movies, and video games. These portrayals often explore the psychological and metaphorical aspects of the creature, delving into themes of isolation, addiction, and the internal struggle between good and evil.

Regardless of its interpretation, the Wendigo remains a powerful and haunting figure in folklore, reminding us of the consequences of our actions and the importance of staying connected to our shared humanity. It serves as a stark reminder that the human spirit is not impervious to darkness and that we must constantly strive to resist the monstrous temptations that lie within. The legend of the Wendigo continues to captivate and terrify, ensuring its place in the annals of folklore for generations to come.

Zombies

The Haitian zombie is rooted in the history and folklore of Haiti, a country rich in spiritual beliefs and practices. Often depicted as a reanimated corpse under the control of a sorcerer, the concept of the zombie has captivated the imaginations of people around the world. To truly understand the history and folklore behind the Haitian zombie, we must delve into the cultural and spiritual traditions of Haiti and explore the various factors that have contributed to the evolution of this enigmatic phenomenon.

One of the key elements in understanding the Haitian zombie is Vodou, an Afro-Haitian religion that blends elements of African spirituality with Catholicism. Vodou has been practiced in Haiti for centuries and is deeply intertwined with the country's history and identity. In Vodou belief, the zombie is not simply a mindless, flesh-eating creature as depicted in popular culture, but rather a person who has been brought back from the dead and enslaved through the use of powerful magic.

The origins of the zombie legend can be traced back to the period of African slavery in Haiti, which lasted from the 16th to the 19th century. During this time, enslaved Africans were ripped from their homes and forced into backbreaking labor on plantations. They were subjected to unimaginable cruelty and exploitation, leading to a deep sense of despair and hopelessness.

In their ancestral African traditions, death was seen as a transition to another realm, and the bodies of the deceased were treated with great reverence. However, in the harsh conditions of slavery, proper burial rituals were often denied to the enslaved Africans. This denial of a dignified afterlife, coupled with the intense suffering experienced during their lives, created a fertile ground for the emergence of the zombie myth.

It is believed that some slave owners in Haiti practiced a form of dark magic known as "bokor" or black magic. These sorcerers were said to possess the ability to reanimate the dead and control them as mindless slaves. By employing a combination of herbs, poisons, and secret rituals, the bokors could induce a state of altered consciousness in their victims, making them appear dead and then reviving them with powerful concoctions.

The concept of the zombie as a tool of control and oppression was a metaphorical expression of the enslaved Africans' plight, illustrating their loss of agency and the stripping away of their humanity. The fear of becoming a zombie became deeply ingrained in the collective consciousness of the Haitian people, symbolizing the horrors of slavery and the abuse of power.

Over time, the zombie legend evolved, capturing the imagination of writers, filmmakers, and storytellers around the world. In the early 20th century, American journalist William Seabrook wrote a sensationalized account of zombies in his book "The Magic Island," introducing the concept to a wider audience. This, coupled with Hollywood's portrayal of zombies as brain-eating monsters, greatly distorted the original Haitian concept.

In recent years, there has been a resurgence of interest in the true roots of the Haitian zombie, with scholars and researchers seeking to separate fact from fiction. Some argue that the zombie is more than just a myth and has a basis in real pharmacological practices. The presence of substances like tetrodotoxin, a potent neurotoxin found in pufferfish, has been suggested as a possible explanation for the zombification process.

However, it is important to approach the topic of zombies with cultural sensitivity and respect for Haitian beliefs and traditions. To the Haitian people, the zombie is not a source of entertainment or fear, but a complex symbol deeply embedded in their history and spirituality.

In conclusion, the history and folklore behind the Haitian zombie are deeply intertwined with the cultural and spiritual traditions of Haiti. Stemming from the horrors of slavery and the oppressive practices of bokors, the zombie emerged as a metaphorical expression of the loss of agency and the stripping away of humanity. While the zombie myth has been sensationalized and distorted over time, it is crucial to appreciate and respect the true roots of this enigmatic figure within the context of Haitian culture and belief systems.